Congressional
Research Service
Informing the legislative debate since 1914 _____

Kuwait: Security, Reform, and U.S. Policy

Kenneth Katzman
Specialist in Middle Eastern Affairs

January 30, 2014

Congressional Research Service

7-5700

www.crs.gov

RS21513

Summary

Kuwait has been pivotal to all the U.S. interventions in the Persian Gulf region since the 1980s because of its location, its role as the object of past Iraqi aggression, and its close cooperation with the United States. Kuwait remains a key to the U.S. ability to act militarily in the northern Persian Gulf region now that all U.S. forces have left Iraq. Kuwait's relations with the post-Saddam government in Iraq have warmed significantly in recent years through resolution of many of the territorial, economic, and political issues from the 1990 Iraqi invasion of Kuwait. Although the threat from Iraq has abated, Kuwait is increasingly suspicious of Iranian intentions in the Gulf, aligning Kuwait with U.S. efforts to contain Iranian power in the Gulf. Still, Kuwait maintains relatively normal economic and political relations with Iran so as not to provoke it to take military action or to provide material support to pro-Iranian elements inside Kuwait. Regional issues were the focus of meeting between the Amir of Kuwait and President Obama on September 13, 2013, during the Amir's visit to Washington, DC.

Domestically, Kuwait's political system has been in turmoil since 2006, taking the form mostly of opposition by many parliamentarians to the political dominance of the Al Sabah family but also broadening to visible public unrest in 2012-13. The disputes have produced repeated constitutional dissolutions of the National Assembly, which trigger new elections, the latest of which were held on July 27, 2013. The July elections followed a six-month period of significant public protests that challenged the Sabah regime's unilateral alteration of election rules to shape the prior elections (December 1, 2012) to its advantage. The July 2013 elections produced a pro-government Assembly more amenable to working with the ruling family, apparently ushering in a period of renewed legislative and governmental action on longstanding issues.

The ruling establishment in Kuwait was able to calm the unrest—although not necessarily eliminate its underlying sources—because the government retains substantial assets. Kuwait remains a relatively wealthy society where most citizens do not want to risk their economic well-being to try to bring about the downfall of Al Sabah rule. Reflecting that sentiment, the opposition has largely confined its demands to limiting Sabah power rather than ending the family's rule. The government has been able to use financial largesse—budgets replete with subsidies and salary increases—as well as some repressive measures as well as legal prosecutions to limit opposition. But, many years of political paralysis have led to economic stagnation, particularly relative to Kuwait's more economically vibrant Gulf neighbors such as Qatar and the United Arab Emirates. The lack of economic vibrancy led to strikes in several economic sectors in 2012.

On regional issues, Kuwait generally acts in partnership with some or all of its allies in the Gulf Cooperation Council (GCC). Kuwait is procuring missile defense technology that furthers the U.S. goal of a GCC-wide missile defense network. On the uprising in Bahrain, in March 2011 Kuwait joined a GCC military intervention on the side of the Bahraini government. Kuwait joined Saudi Arabia and UAE in supporting the decision of the Egyptian military in July 2013 to remove elected president and senior Muslim Brotherhood leader Mohammad Morsi from power. Kuwait supports the Sunni-led rebellion in Syria, although Kuwait has largely confined its support for rebellion to humanitarian and financial aid. Kuwait has tended to defer to de facto GCC leader Saudi Arabia in offering proposals to resolve the Israeli-Palestinian dispute.

Contents

Figures

Tables

Contacts

Government and Political Reform[1]

Kuwait's optimism after the 2003 fall of its nemesis, Saddam Hussein, soured after the January 15, 2006, death of Amir (ruler) Jabir Ahmad al-Jabir Al Sabah. Since then, Kuwait has lurched from one political crisis to the next, producing a sense of economic and political stagnation. At the time of Amir Jabir's death, his successor, Shaykh Sa'ad bin Abdullah Al Sabah, was very ill (he later died), and a brief succession dispute among rival branches of the ruling Al Sabah family ensued. It was resolved with Prime Minister Shaykh Sabah al-Ahmad al-Jabir Al Sabah becoming Amir on January 29, 2006; about 83, he is the younger brother of the late Amir. The succession dispute was unprecedented in Kuwait and the broader Gulf region for the first use of an elected legislature's constitutional ability to remove a leader.

Although the leadership question was resolved, it produced a suspension of the tacit agreement to alternate succession between the Jabir and Salem branches of the family. Amir Sabah appointed two members of his Jabir branch as Crown Prince/heir apparent and as prime minister (Shaykh Nawwaf al-Ahmad Al Sabah and Shaykh Nasser al Muhammad al-Ahmad Al Sabah respectively). The highest-ranking member of the Salem branch in the government was Dr. Mohammad Al Sabah, deputy prime minister and foreign minister. Both resigned or were replaced in 2011.Tensions between the two branches of the family have since simmered, and no permanent alternative power-sharing mechanism has been reached. The governmental infighting provided rationale and additional political space for various youth and other reform-oriented groups inspired by the Arab uprisings that began in early 2011.

Government Structure

The Amir is the head of state and ruler of Kuwait. He appoints a Prime Minister, as head of government, who in turn appoints a cabinet. The Prime Minister has always been a member of the Sabah family, and until 2003 the Prime Minister also was Crown Prince/heir apparent. In recent years, there has been discussion within the Sabah family of restoring the concurrency of the Prime Minister and Crown Prince position because the National Assembly is not able, constitutionally, to question the Crown Prince. In typical Kuwaiti cabinets, three out of four deputy prime ministers are members of the family, as is the Defense Minister, Foreign Minister, and Interior Minister. Each Kuwaiti cabinet has typically had at least a few family members heading other ministries as well. The Prime Minister is Shaykh Jabir al-Mubarak Al Sabah, who took office in December 4, 2011, and was reappointed following the July 2013 elections. The cabinet has 28 ministers, plus a Central Bank governor.

The Amir has additional broad powers. He serves as Commander-in-Chief of the Armed Forces, and all judges. The Amir, as noted below, has the power to suspend the National Assembly for limited periods of time, and to commute prison sentences. Kuwait's Amirs can be as involved or disengaged from day-to-day governance as they choose; Amir Sabah tends to be more directly involved in governance than was his predecessor.

---

[1] Much of this section is from the State Department's country report on human rights practices for 2012 (released April 19, 2013), http://www.state.gov/j/drl/rls/hrrpt/humanrightsreport/index htm?year=2012&dlid=204370#wrapper; the *International Religious Freedom Report* for 2012 (May 20, 2013), http://www.state.gov/j/drl/rls/irf/religiousfreedom/index htm?year=2012&dlid=208398#wrapper; and the *Trafficking in Persons Report for 2013* (June 19, 2013), http://www.state.gov/documents/organization/210740.pdf.

The National Assembly and Disputes With the Ruling Family

The National Assembly, established by Kuwait's November 1962 constitution, is the longest-serving all-elected body among the Gulf monarchies. Fifty seats are elected, and up to 16 members of the cabinet serve in the Assembly *ex-officio*.

Assembly Authorities

Although Kuwait's constitution enshrines the hereditary monarchy, the Kuwait National Assembly has more scope of authority than any legislative or consultative body in the Persian Gulf. It can introduce legislation as well as consider and vote on government-introduced legislation. The Assembly does not have the power to confirm cabinet nominees (individually or en bloc), but it can, by simple majority of elected members, vote "no confidence" and thereby remove individual ministers. When the Assembly takes that step, it generally does so after parliamentary questioning of that minister, referred to as "grilling." The Assembly can vote no confidence in the prime minister by voting "inability to cooperate with the government," and it can veto government decrees issued during periods of Assembly suspension. Amirs of Kuwait have, on several occasions (1976-1981, 1986-1992, 2003, 2006, 2008, 2009, 2011, and 2012), used their constitutional authority to dissolve the Assembly when it grilled or threatened to grill government ministers. Suspension of the Assembly mandates new elections within 60 days.

Those opposing the government have tended to seek greater authority for the Assembly and a limitation of the powers of the government and by extension, limitations of the political and economic power of the Al Sabah. The opposition, in general, seeks a constitutional monarchy in which the Assembly, or an elected majority faction within the Assembly, names a Prime Minister who in turn assembles a cabinet.

Voter Eligibility

For at least two decades, voter eligibility has been a closely watched indicator of Kuwait's political liberalization. The government has expanded the electorate gradually; in the 1990s, the government extended the vote to sons of naturalized Kuwaitis and Kuwaitis naturalized for at least 20 (as opposed to 30) years. The long deadlock on female suffrage began to break in May 2004, after the government submitted to the Assembly a bill to give women the right to vote and run. (A government attempt in May 1999 to institute female suffrage by decree was vetoed by the Assembly.) In May 2005, then Prime Minister Shaykh Sabah (now Amir) pressed the Assembly to adopt the government bill, which it did on May 16, 2005 (35-23); the bill was effective as of the 2006 National Assembly elections.

Political Factions in and Outside the National Assembly

Political parties are still not permitted, but factions are organized and compete in Assembly elections as "currents," "trends," or "political societies." Many of these factions meet and plan their strategies at a parallel Kuwaiti tradition called *diwaniyyas*—informal social gatherings, held at night, held by elites of all political ideologies and backgrounds. There are a growing number of *diwaniyyas* organized by women. Factions in Kuwait, both in and outside the National Assembly, are often fluid, but in general they group as follows:

The "Opposition"

- *"Liberals."* Highly educated elites who tend to form the core of the opposition to the government. Many of the liberals had been part of Arab nationalist movements in the 1960s and 1970s, and in many cases have studied abroad. In prior years they had operated under the banner "Kuwait Democratic Forum." Some liberal Kuwaitis often side with the government.

- *Sunni Islamists.* They are generally opposed to the government. Within this broad category, there are two major groupings: those linked to the Muslim Brotherhood, and harder line Sunnis called Salafists. Those linked to the Muslim Brotherhood have often operated under a banner called the Islamic Constitutional Movement (ICM).

- *Youths and Intellectuals.* The broader opposition, outside the National Assembly, the opposition includes youth and intellectuals, many of whom have become more active since the Arab uprisings began in early 2011 but have been active in Kuwait far longer than that. Since 2008, these groups have sometimes organized during election campaigns to support liberal deputies, using such names as the "Orange Movement" or "Fifth Fence."

Government Supporters

- *"Tribalists."* Generally less educated but who dominate two out of the five electoral districts and tend to support the government, although not universally. At times, some tribalists in the Assembly have grouped into a faction widely referred to as "service deputies"—Assembly members primarily focused on steering government largesse and patronage to their constituents.

- *Shiites.* Most in the Assembly are Islamists, assembled in a bloc called the National Islamic Alliance. They tend to side with the government, perhaps out of greater concern about Sunni Islamists.

- *Women.* When in the Assembly, women, both Shiite and Sunni, have tended to align with the government. Many women outside the Assembly, however, have participated in opposition demonstrations.

Post-2006 Political Crises: Assembly Suspensions and Elections

The post-2006 political deadlock has manifested as repeated Assembly suspensions and subsequent elections, none of which has resolved fundamental differences over the power balance between the executive and the legislature. Five months after becoming leader, Amir Sabah suspended the Assembly in May 2006 when 29 opposition members demanded to question the Prime Minister over the government's refusal to reduce the number of electoral districts to five (from 25). The opposition wanted the larger districts to make it more difficult to influence the outcome through "vote buying" or tribal politics.

Elections During 2006 - 2009

- *June 29, 2006 election.* In this election, the opposition, which attracted youth support under the "Orange" banner, won 34 out of the 50 seats. The election was the first in which women could vote or run, but none of the 27 women candidates won. After the election, the Amir accepted demands to reduce the number of electoral districts to five and a law to implement that change, as of the next election, took effect.

- *May 17, 2008 Election.* The schisms between the opposition and the government produced another crisis in March 2008 when the Assembly insisted on pay raises for state employees as a response to spiraling inflation. The government refused, the cabinet resigned, and the Amir dissolved the Assembly and set new elections for May 17, 2008. Perhaps benefitting from the move from 25 to 5 electoral districts, Sunni Islamists and conservative tribal leaders won a total of 24 seats— an increase of 4. Their allies—the so-called "liberals"—won seven seats. Shiites increased their representation by one, to a total of five seats. Pro-government and other independent tribalists held the remaining 14 seats. As in the 2006 election, none of the 27 women candidates was elected. After the appointment of a post-election cabinet appointments, Islamists agitated unsuccessfully against the appointment of two female ministers. And, Sunni-Shiite tensions added to the dissension within the Kuwaiti elite, possibly as a spillover of sectarian tensions in post-Saddam Iraq. In November 2008, the cabinet resigned when three Sunni Assembly deputies requested to question the Prime Minister about suspected corruption and his permitting the visit of a radical Iranian Shiite cleric. The Amir subsequently reappointed Shaykh Nasser as Prime Minister and did not suspend the Assembly.

- *May 16, 2009 Election.* The power struggle between the government and opposition Assembly deputies flared again in March 2009 when the Assembly insisted on questioning the Prime Minister on his handling of the global financial crisis and alleged misuse of public funds. On March 19, 2009, the Amir suspended the Assembly, triggering elections held on May 16, 2009. Turnout was relatively light at about 55% of the 385,000 eligible voters, and produced more than 20 new parliamentarians, including 4 women—the first to be elected. They included Masouma Mubarak, mentioned above (a Shiite); Rola Dashti, who had been narrowly defeated in 2006; and professors Aseel al-Awadhi and Salwa al-Jassar. In December 2009, Assembly members questioned Prime Minister Shaykh Nasser for corruption in the earlier 2008 elections; this marked the first time in the Gulf region that a head of government had appeared before an elected body. On December 17, 2009, a new election was avoided when deputies voted 35-13 to express confidence in him. But, one year later, security forces broke up a demonstration by parliamentarians and civil society activists against government attempts to limit National Assembly powers. Shaykh Nasser narrowly survived a no-confidence vote on January 5, 2011 (22 of the 50 Assembly deputies supported the motion), [2] which some saw as indicating that the government had lost support among tribalist from the outer districts of Kuwait City, which are inhabited by generally less affluent, naturalized citizens. [3]

---

[2] "Kuwait's Prime Minister Survives Parliament Vote." *Al Jazeera TV*, January 5, 2011.

[3] Kristin Smith Diwan, "Kuwait: Too Much Politics, or Not Enough?," *Foreign Policy* online, January 10, 2011.

2011: Arab Uprisings Add to Kuwait's Political Crises

The Arab uprisings that began in early 2011 affected Kuwait by broadening the opposition beyond the National Assembly and other elites. After the vote, opposition deputies, supported by youths under a banner called the "Fifth Fence," and who were inspired by the Arab uprisings, called for the resignation of Interior Minister Jabir al-Khalid Al Sabah for failing to prevent the alleged torturing to death of a man in custody. In advance of a February 8, 2011, public protest planned to coincide with his questioning by the Assembly, the Interior Minister resigned. The Fifth Fence postponed the planned protest until March 8, 2011, but it attracted only a few hundred participants. That same month, Shiite parliamentarian Saleh Ashour asked to question the Foreign Minister about Kuwait's sending of naval forces as part of the GCC military intervention to support Bahrain's government—a decision many Kuwaiti Shiites opposed as unjustly supporting the Sunni Bahraini monarchy. Rather than face the questioning, the cabinet resigned. Prime Minister Nasser was re-appointed to a caretaker government, and a new cabinet, with only the Oil and Commerce ministers changing, was formed on May 8, 2011 (the seventh cabinet formed by Shaykh Nasser since he became Prime Minister).

The government came under renewed popular pressure in September 2011 following reports that two of Kuwait's largest banks had deposited $92 million into the accounts of two National Assembly members. The transfers, including those to seven other parliamentarians, suggested that the government had sought to buy the loyalty of parliamentarians. Thousands of Kuwait protesters to take to the streets on September 21, 2011 to call for the resignation of the Prime Minister. Two days later, an estimated 10,000 demonstrators demanded the Prime Minister's resignation. Probably as a direct response to the allegations, on September 25, 2011, the cabinet adopted an anti-corruption draft law.

The protests were accompanied by strikes in the oil industry and the state-run banking and health care industry in September 2011. However, these job actions did not appear directly related to the political disputes, but rather to disputes over pay, benefits, and working conditions.

2012-2013: Cycle of Frequent Elections and Demonstrations

The 2011-2012 National Assembly opened in October 2011 with continued recriminations. Opposition deputies boycotted committee meetings, and moderate liberals joined opposition deputies to give the opposition enough votes for a successful no-confidence motion against the prime minister. On November 16, 2011, oppositionists in and outside the Assembly, including the Fifth Fence, forced their way into the Assembly building and demanded the Prime Minister's resignation. The Amir issued a decree tightening security at the building, but the political pressure continued and on November 28, 2011, Prime Minister Nasser resigned.

Amir Switches Prime Ministers

Rather than reappointing Shaykh Nasser as a caretaker, the Amir appointed another royal family member, then-Defense Minister Shaykh Jabir al-Mubarak Al Sabah, as Prime Minister. He was sworn in, but without first naming a new cabinet, on December 4, 2011. Two days later, on December 6, 2011, he recommended—and Amir Sabah concurred—dissolution of the National Assembly and new elections. The country started preparing for Assembly elections set for February 2, 2012 (within the constitutionally mandated 60 days).

Subsequently, opposition deputies began nominating themselves as candidates. Primary elections are formally banned, although some tribes hold informal "tribal primaries" to determine who their candidate will be. On December 6, 2011, a group of 20 opposition deputies announced they would compete as one "Opposition Bloc." Opposition youth leaders announced they would back opposition deputies who would push for a fully elected government in which the prime minister is selected by the Assembly, legalization of political parties, and election law changes. Such announcements confirmed the fears of the royal family that dissolving the Assembly and holding new elections would empower oppositionists sympathetic to the 2011 Arab uprisings. However, refusing to call a new election would have portrayed the government as attempting to cover up its alleged corruption. Some secular oppositionists feared that a new election would increase the ranks of Islamist deputies, who are well organized.

February 2, 2012, Election And Aftermath

Many of the mainstream predictions appeared to be realized in the February 2, 2012, election. As shown in **Table 1** below, groups opposed to the government won at least 32 of the 50 seats. Islamist groups increased their influence markedly and they and their allies who oppose the government took control of the Assembly's agenda. They benefitted at the expense of the pro-government independent deputies who were defeated decisively, many of whom were the Assembly members alleged to have received government funds in the scandal discussed above. Kuwaiti liberals lost support and, in a blow to secular Kuwaitis, none of the 19 women who ran, including the 4 incumbents, was elected. Turnout was about 62%, slightly higher than the 2009 election. A leading opposition figure, Ahmad al-Sadun, a previous speaker (1985-1999), returned to that post when the Assembly convened in February 2012, replacing the relatively pro-government Jassim Al-Khurafi, a major figure in Kuwait's merchant community.

The new government formed after the election was again headed by Prime Minister Shaykh Jabir al-Mubarak Al Sabah. He appointed 10 new ministers and retained the remainder. No women were appointed. The government refused opposition demands to appoint oppositionists to at least nine cabinet positions, appointing instead four such ministers. And, as expected, the new Assembly immediately asserted itself: in March 2012, Shiite deputy Ashour filed a successful motion to question the prime minister about alleged failure to fully investigate official corruption allegations—an issue that had caused the Central Bank governor to resign in February 2012. The Prime Minister was questioned on March 28, 2012, but opponents did not file a vote of no-confidence motion. With the Assembly insisting on "grilling" the Interior Minister, on June 18, 2012, the Amir exercised his prerogative under Article 106 of the constitution to suspend the Assembly for one month—a temporary suspension renewable for another two months (but with the concurrence of the Assembly). The suspension extended almost to the holy month of Ramadan, at which time the Assembly is not in session anyway, meaning the Assembly would be closed until October 2012.

Second Election in 2012 Triggered by Court Decision

On June 20, 2012, Kuwait's constitutional court ruled that the December 2011 suspension was not conducted in accordance with the constitution, on the grounds that a new cabinet had not been sworn in before the Amir's suspension was ordered. The court ordered the previous (elected in May 2009) Assembly reinstated. However, the ruling increased political turmoil in Kuwait and the "reinstated" 2009 Assembly did not meet at all.

The government requested the constitutional court revisit the number of election districts—a motion that its critics said was a prelude to gerrymandering districts to ensure a pro-government majority. The court ruled against the government on September 26, 2012, and, on October 8, 2012, the Amir formally disbanded the National Assembly under the constitution. He later set a new election date of December 1, 2012, and simultaneously issued a decree altering the election law to allow voters in each district to vote for only one candidate—not the four per district in prior law. The Amir's decision—announced as an effort to avoid chaos produced by the continued government-Assembly power struggle—was seen by the opposition as an effort to complicate opposition efforts to forge alliances in each district. Some observers said the Amir's election decree did not necessarily favor any side—in part because the opposition could benefit from "one man one vote" just as easily as the government could. According to many observers, opposition anger at the decree was fueled mainly by the perception of the Amir's arbitrary exercise of power.

The opposition rallied against the revised election rules—on October 21, 2012, it held an unprecedented demonstration, consisting of an estimated 50,000-150,000 Kuwaitis marching toward the iconic Kuwait Towers landmark. The demonstration was suppressed by security forces; there were injuries reported, but no deaths. Some parliamentarians and even some younger members of the Sabah family were arrested. Smaller demonstrations took place subsequently, including one held on October 31, 2012, calling for the freeing of outspoken oppositionist Musallam al-Barrak, a former parliamentarian who was arrested on October 15, 2012, for allegedly insulting the Amir. On November 2, 2012, following a night of clashes between protesters and security forces, the government announced it would enforce an October 2012 ban on gatherings of over 20 persons.

The government went forward with the vote, under the Amir's controversial election decree. The government reported turnout of about 40% of the approximately 400,000 eligible voters. Because the opposition boycotted the vote, the election produced an Assembly overwhelming "pro-government" largely on the strength of the seventeen pro-government Shiites elected—including five Islamist Shiites of the National Islamic Alliance. The number of Shiite deputies elected was double that in any prior Assembly. Three females, including Masouma Mubarak, were elected. Some Sunni Islamists were elected, but—with the exception of two in the Salafi grouping—they were generally not affiliated with the Sunni Islamist political societies that have been present in the Assembly for decades.

On December 5, 2012, the Amir asked Prime Minister Shaykh Jabir Mubarak to form a new cabinet. The opposition continued demonstrating to try to force change on the Al Sabah, and demonstrations, some of them large, subsequently became a relatively regular occurrence in Kuwait. Still, the government tried to move forward on long stalled legislation with a solidly supportive Assembly. One bill that was enacted by the Assembly on March 20, 2013, gives about 4,000 "bidoons" (stateless residents, discussed below) citizenship.

Another Court-Triggered Election in July 2013

Even though the election took place, the Amir's election decree remained under legal challenge. On June 16, 2013, the Constitutional Court ruled that the Amir's decree that each person would vote for only one candidate (reduced from four) was constitutional, but the court dissolved the Assembly on the basis of improper technicalities in the Amir's election decree. The government subsequently set new elections (the sixth election in five years) for July 27, 2013. A total of 418 candidates registered, of which 8 were female. Some opposition societies, including those linked to the Muslim Brotherhood, announced a boycott but other opposition groups announced they would participate.

The turnout in the July 27, 2013, vote was about 52%, according to the government and independent observers. The vote produced a decidedly pro-government Assembly, with the Muslim Brotherhood opposition absent and a few Salafi Islamists. Pro-government deputies in the Assembly include a broad range of groups and reflect successful government outreach to the tribalists, and cooptation of many liberals. The government is less reliant on Shiite deputies than in the previous Assembly, with Shiite deputies numbering eight (down from 15)—close to their long term average in the Assembly. Increasing sectarian splits between Sunnis and Shiites in the region had caused many Kuwaitis to resent the high number of Shiites in the previous Assembly. The current National Assembly speaker is Marzuq al-Ghanim, the nephew of former speaker al-Khurafi.

Post-Election Cabinet. A new cabinet was named on August 4, 2013. Shaykh Jabir remained Prime Minister, and he retained much of the previous cabinet. Among significant changes, Shaykh Khalid al-Hamad Al Sabah was promoted to first deputy prime minister and Minister of Foreign Affairs. A former head of domestic intelligence (National Security Bureau), Shaykh Mohammad Khalid Al Sabah, was made Minister of Interior. Lieutenant General Khalid Al Jarrah Al Sabah, formerly chief of staff of the Kuwaiti army, entered the government as Minister of Defense. The cabinet included two Shiites and two females: former Assembly deputy Rola Dashti holds Minister of State portfolios for Planning and for National Assembly Affairs. Thikra al-Rashidi is Minister of Social Affairs and Labor. However, on January 7, 2014, the Prime Minister reshuffled the cabinet to improve relations with the National Assembly: he removed the two female ministers and replaced only one of them (Ms. Rashidi) with another female (Minister of Social Affairs and Labor Hind al-Sabih). He replaced a member of the ruling family (Shaykh Salem Abd al-Aziz Al Sabah) as Finance Minister with Anas al-Salih, who is well known to the business community. He replaced the Minister of Oil with Ali al-Umair, a Salafist parliamentarian (one of two parliamentarians in the cabinet). He reduced the number of Shiite cabinet members to one—Yasser Abul as Minister of Housing—housing has polled as a major issue among Kuwaitis. That brought the total Islamists in the cabinet to four, from two –all of whom are from the Salafist faction and not the Muslim Brotherhood current.

Since the election, even though leading opposition figures are outside the Assembly rather than working within the system, there have been no major public demonstrations. Opposition demands remain confined to calls for a constitutional monarchy, in which the elected parliament selects the cabinet. However, some experts maintain that protests might revive if the government continues to arrest opposition activists who criticize the Amir on social media.

Table 1. Composition of the National Assembly: 2008–2013

Ideology/Affiliation	Post-2008 Election	Post-2009 Vote	Post-Feb. 2012 Vote	Post December 2012 Vote	Post July 2103 Vote
Sunni Islamist (Muslim Brotherhood and Salafi, including tribalists. generally opposes the government)	24	14	23	4	3 (all Salafi, no Muslim Brotherhood)
Liberals (generally opposition)	7	8	5	1	9
Popular Action Bloc (generally opposition)	0	2	4	0	0
Shiite (generally pro-government)	5	9	7	17	8
Sunni Independents (includes tribalists, pro-business deputies and women). Generally pro-government	14	17	11	28	30
Women (generally pro-government)	0	4	0	3	2
Included in categories above					

Source: CRS, based on articles and analysis from various observers.

Note: Some members of the National Assembly might span several different categories and several sources often disagree on precise categorizations of the members of the Assembly.

U.S. Responses and Implications for U.S. Interests

There has been no alteration of the U.S.-Kuwait relationship as a result of Kuwait's handling of 2011-2013 unrest. On October 23, 2012—following the large protest discussed above—the State Department said the United States "call[s] on all sides to exercise restraint," and indirectly criticized the government's ban on large public gatherings. The official statements following President Obama's meeting with Amir Sabah at the White House on September 13, 2013, did not indicate that the political situation in Kuwait was discussed in depth.[4] Nor has unrest caused an interruption or alteration to U.S. democracy programs in Kuwait. These programs, funded from the Middle East Partnership Initiative (MEPI) and other U.S. assistance accounts, included discussions with Kuwaiti leaders, public diplomacy, building civil society, enhancing the capabilities of independent Kuwaiti media, promoting women's rights, and providing a broad spectrum of educational opportunities.

However, as an example of potential implications for the United States of unrest in Kuwait, in September 2012 some Kuwaiti Islamist parliamentarians called for a demonstration outside the U.S. Embassy in Kuwait to condemn the "Innocence of Muslims" video produced privately in the United States. The parliamentarians who attended the protest withdrew from it after some demonstrators called for storming the Embassy. The Embassy was not attacked.

---

[4] http://www.whitehouse.gov/the-press-office/2013/09/13/remarks-president-obama-and-amir-sabah-al-sabah-kuwait-after-bilateral-m.

Broader Human Rights Issues[5]

On broader human rights issues, the latest State Department Country Report on Human Rights Practices for 2012, released April 19, 2013, largely reiterated the criticisms of previous reports. In May 2011, Kuwait took over Syria's bid for a seat on the U.N. Human Rights Council.

Women's Rights

Women have made significant strides in achieving their rights in Kuwait over the past several years, as exemplified by their running and winning election to the National Assembly. However, the election of women has not translated into an expansion of women in the cabinet. There have rarely been more than two women in the 28 person cabinet, and only one in the cabinet named in January 2014. As discussed above, two women were elected in the July 2013 election. In September 2012, the Higher Judicial Council appointed seven women as public prosecutors, a decision that drew strong criticism from Kuwaiti Islamists.

More broadly, women in Kuwait can drive, unlike their counterparts in neighboring Saudi Arabia. There are several nongovernmental organizations run by Kuwaiti women, such as the Kuwait Women's Cultural and Social Society, that are dedicated to improving rights for women and to agitating on several different issues unrelated to gender. Still, women are subject to a broad array of discriminatory practices and abuses. The law does not specifically prohibit domestic violence, although courts try such cases as assault. Successive State Department and outside human rights reports have asserted that violence particularly against expatriate women working in domestic service roles is frequent. Some expatriate women have also been subjected to nonpayment of wages and withholding of passports.[6] Kuwaiti women who marry non-Kuwaiti men cannot give their spouses or children Kuwaiti citizenship.

Trafficking in Persons

Kuwait was, for the sixth year in a row, designated by the State Department's *Trafficking in Persons* report for 2013 (issued June 19, 2013, cited earlier) in "Tier Three" (worst level). The designation has been maintained because, according to the 2013 report, Kuwait is "not making sufficient efforts" to comply with minimum standards for the elimination of trafficking. The report notes that Kuwait adopted an anti-trafficking law in March 2013, but did not demonstrate significant efforts to prosecute and convict trafficking offenders and there is no lead national anti-trafficking coordinating body.

Status of "Bidoons" and Other Expatriates

Non-Gulf Arabs and Asians, and approximately 106,000 stateless residents (known as "bidoons") continue to face discrimination. The government asserts that the bidoons deliberately destroyed evidence of another nationality in order to obtain generous social benefits in Kuwait. Despite that suspicion, in October 2010 the government promised to implement a plan to resolve the legal and

---

[5] Much of this section is from the State Department's country report on human rights practices for 2012 (released April 19, 2013), http://www.state.gov/j/drl/rls/hrrpt/humanrightsreport/index htm?year=2012&dlid=204370#wrapper; and the Human Rights Watch World Report for 2014. Released January 2014.

[6] Fahim, Kareem. "Away From Home, Fleeing Domestic Life." *New York Times*, August 2, 2010.

economic status of the bidoons. The lack of action contributed to a March 11, 2011 demonstration by bidoons. Following that demonstration, the government set up a "Central System for Remedying the Status of Illegal Residents," with a mandate to resolve the status of the bidoons within five years. During 2011, the government granted citizenship to several hundred bidoons. The National Assembly passed a law in March 2013 to give an additional 4,000 bidoons citizenship. On the other hand, on September 20, 2012, security forces raided a suburb of Kuwait City and arrested over 2,100 persons. The detainees were alleged violators of residency laws, mostly Asians.

Freedom of Expression and Media Freedoms

Official press censorship ended in 1992, assisting the growth of a vibrant press, but successive State Department human rights reports have asserted that the government does not always respect the constitutional provisions for freedom of speech and the press. The government monitors Internet communications for defamation and security reasons. And, by law, newspaper publishers must be licensed by the Ministry of Information.

Kuwait's penal code (Article 25) provides for up to five years in jail for "objecting to the rights and authorities of the Amir or faulting him," and the government has made increasing use of this provision to quiet opponents. Since 2012, the Public Prosecution Office has charged about 40 Kuwaitis with faulting the Amir for criticizing him on Twitter, Facebook, or other media. In March 2012, a Kuwaiti court suspended the Kuwaiti newspaper *Al Dar* for publishing articles that insulted Shiites and therefore could incite sectarian strife. In April 2012, Kuwaiti writer Mohammad al-Mulaifi was sentenced to seven years in prison for writing on Twitter about sectarian divisions in Kuwait. Five persons charged with faulting the Amir" were acquitted in February 2013, but in July 2013 an appeals court overturned the conviction of three former Assembly deputies on that charge. The same court upheld a 20 month sentence of Sarra al-Darees for Twitter messages "tarnishing the Amir's authority." In mid-April 2013, outspoken former parliamentarian Musallam al-Barrak, mentioned earlier - a figure many consider de-facto "opposition leader - was sentenced to five years in prison for insulting the Amir; his sentence was overturned on May 27, 2013. In November 2013, a Kuwaiti court sentenced a Kuwait man to five years in prison for a Twitter comment about Sunni and Shiite theology. On December 2013, the Constitutional Court rejected a challenged to Article 25 of the penal code.

Labor Rights

The law protects the right of workers to form and join unions, conduct legal strikes, and bargain collectively, but contains significant restrictions. The government allows one trade union per occupation, but the only legal trade federation is the Kuwait Trade Union Federation (KTUF). Foreign workers, with the exception of domestic workers, are allowed to join unions, and the government has tended not to impede strikes. On October 10, 2011, about 3,000 customs officers went on strike demanding higher wages and better working conditions; the action caused a temporary halt to Kuwaiti oil exports. On October 26, 2011, the government criticized the strikes as "tantamount to attacks on the state's status, sovereignty, its interests, and its citizens," and "cannot be tolerated." In early 2012, strikes briefly grounded state-owned Kuwait Airways, and there have been occasional small strikes since.

Religious Freedom

The State Department religious freedom report for 2012 (released May 20, 2013), cited earlier, reported that the "trend" in the government's respect for religious freedom "did not change significantly" during 2012. Shiite Muslims (about 30% of Kuwait's population) continue to report official discrimination, including limited access to religious education and the perceived government unwillingness to permit the building of new Shiite mosques. Unlike in Bahrain, Shiites are well represented in the police force and the military/security apparatus, although they generally are not offered leadership positions in those institutions. On the other hand, in early April 2012, the Kuwaiti ministry that oversees houses of worship said it will begin monitoring Shiite mourning houses known as *Husseiniyas*, but it also stated that it is considering providing state funds to Shiite mosques, as it does for Sunni mosques. On June 6, 2012, the Amir refused to sign (vetoed) a National Assembly bill stipulating the death penalty for those who curse the major figures and symbols of Islam, including the Quran.

Kuwait has seven officially recognized Christian churches to serve the approximately 450,000 Christians (mostly foreign residents) in Kuwait. However, Islamists in the National Assembly have sometimes sought to prevent the building of new churches in Kuwait.[7] Members of religions not sanctioned in the Quran—including about 400 Baha'i's, 100,000 Buddhists, 600,000 Hindus, and 10,000 Sikhs—are mostly non-citizens working in Kuwait and have not been allowed to operate official places of worship. They have been permitted to worship in their homes.

U.S.-Kuwait Relations and Defense Cooperation

Kuwait has been a pivotal partner of the United States through three Gulf wars: the Iran-Iraq War, the 1991 Persian Gulf War, and the 2003 U.S.-led war to oust Saddam Hussein. In all three cases, Kuwait's security was directly at stake. U.S. officials stress that Kuwait went to extraordinary lengths to support U.S. policy and operations, even though Kuwait did not contribute forces to the U.S.-led stabilization operations in post-Taliban Afghanistan or post-Saddam Iraq.

A U.S. consulate was opened in Kuwait in October 1951; it was elevated to an embassy upon Kuwait's independence from Britain in 1961. Kuwait, the first Gulf state to establish relations with the Soviet Union in the 1960s, was not particularly close to the United States until the Iran-Iraq War (1980-1988).

Cooperation During the 1980-1988 Iran-Iraq War

Kuwait and the United States grew politically and militarily close during that war because of its spillover to Kuwait. Through intimidation, Iran sought to compel Kuwait not to support Iraq in that war. Iran fired at and struck some Kuwaiti oil facilities, including the Al Ahmadi terminal, with Silkworm surface-to-surface missiles. In 1987-1988, the United States established a U.S. naval escort and tanker reflagging program to protect Kuwaiti and international shipping from Iranian naval attacks (Operation Earnest Will). As part of the skirmishes between the United

---

[7] Middle East Media Research Institute. "In Kuwait, Public Debate Over Demand to Demolish Churches," April 10, 2012.

States and Iran in the course of that operation, Iran attacked a Kuwaiti oil installation (Sea Island terminal).

Defense Cooperation Agreement (DCA) Follows "Operation Desert Storm"

Believing Saddam Hussein would reward Kuwait for assisting Iraq financially and logistically during the Iran-Iraq War, Kuwait's leaders were shaken by the August 2, 1990, Iraqi invasion. Iraq's public justification was an accusation that Kuwait was overproducing oil and thereby harming Iraq's ability to repay its debts and recover economically from the long war with Iran. However, most experts believe that the invasion was a result of Saddam's intent to dominate the Persian Gulf politically, economically, and militarily. Iraq's occupation lasted until a U.S.-led coalition forces of nearly 500,000 expelled Iraqi forces from Kuwait in "Operation Desert Storm" (January 16, 1991 - February 28, 1991). Kuwait's leaders, who spent the occupation period in Saudi Arabia, were restored to power in Kuwait. Kuwait contributed financially to the 1991 war —it paid $16.059 billion to offset the U.S. incremental costs of Desert Shield/Desert Storm.

The U.S.-led expulsion of Iraqi forces from Kuwait led to a deepening of the U.S.-Kuwait security relationship, the cornerstone of which was a broad 10-year Defense Cooperation Agreement (DCA) signed on September 19, 1991 for an initial 10-year period. The DCA remains in effect.[8] Although the text is classified, the pact reportedly provides for mutual discussions in the event of a crisis; joint military exercises; U.S. evaluation of, advice to, and training of Kuwaiti forces; U.S. arms sales; prepositioning of U.S. military equipment; and U.S. access to a range of Kuwaiti facilities. These facilities include: Ali al-Salem Air Base; the main U.S. headquarters in Kuwait at Camp Arifjan (40 miles south of Kuwait City); a desert training base and firing range called Camp Buehring, far out in the desert, near the border with Saudi Arabia; and a naval facility called Camp Patriot.[9] Under the DCA, enough U.S. armor to outfit a brigade is pre-positioned in at Camp Arifjan; the equipment was used for the 2003 invasion of Iraq and returned after the U.S. mission in Iraq ended. U.S. forces vacated Camp Doha, the headquarters for U.S. forces in Kuwait during the 1990s, in December 2005. The DCA includes a Status of Forces Agreement (SOFA) provides that U.S. forces in Kuwait be subject to U.S. rather than Kuwaiti law—a common feature of such arrangements.

Kuwait's cooperation under the DCA was pivotal to U.S. and allied efforts to contain Saddam Hussein after the 1991 war. U.S. forces used Kuwaiti facilities to conduct containment operations, including the 1992-2003 enforcement of a "no fly zone" over southern Iraq (Operation Southern Watch). This operation involved 1,000 U.S. Air Force personnel in Kuwait, mostly at Kuwait air bases. As a deterrent to Iraq, as noted above, the United States prepositioned armor in Kuwait, there were generally about 4,000 or more U.S. troops stationed in Kuwait at any given time during the 1990s. Kuwait contributed about $350 million per year for U.S. military costs of these containment operations. Kuwait also funded two-thirds of the $51 million per year U.N. budget for the 1991-2003 Iraq-Kuwait Observer Mission (UNIKOM) that monitored the Iraq-Kuwait border. Kuwait hosted an additional 5,000 U.S. forces during the major combat phases of Operation Enduring Freedom, which ousted the Taliban from power in Afghanistan.

---

[8] http://www.whitehouse.gov/the-press-office/2013/09/13/remarks-president-obama-and-amir-sabah-al-sabah-kuwait-after-bilateral-m.

[9] Hajjar, Sami. U.S. Military Presence in the Gulf: Challenges and Prospects. U.S. Army War College, Strategic Studies Institute. p. 27.

Major Non-NATO Ally Designation

Recognizing Kuwait's consistent and multi-faceted cooperation, particularly with U.S. operations in Iraq, on April 1, 2004, the Bush Administration designated Kuwait as a "major non-NATO ally (MNNA)," a designation held by only one other Gulf state (Bahrain). Afghanistan obtained that designation in 2012. The designation opens Kuwait to buy the same U.S. equipment that is sold to U.S. allies in NATO.

Supporting the U.S. Ousting of Saddam and Stabilization Mission: 2003-11

Because Saddam Hussein had invaded Kuwait, Kuwait enthusiastically supported the Bush Administration's decision to militarily overthrow Saddam Hussein (Operation Iraqi Freedom [OIF]). It hosted the vast bulk of the U.S. invasion force of about 250,000 forces, as well as the other coalition troops that entered Iraq. To secure that force, Kuwait closed off its entire northern half for weeks before the invasion. It also allowed U.S. use of two air bases, its international airport, and sea ports; and provided $266 million in burden sharing support to the combat, including base support, personnel support, and supplies such as food and fuel.

In order to promote Iraqi stability after the fall of Saddam Hussein, Kuwait took a number of major steps: it built a water line into Iraq, and it ran a humanitarian operation center (HOC) that gave over $550 million in assistance to Iraqis from 2003-2011. A Kuwaiti company, First Kuwaiti General Trading and Contracting, was lead contractor on the large U.S. embassy in Iraq that opened in January 2009. On April 22, 2008, Kuwait hosted a regional conference on Iraq's stability, which included the United States, Iran, and other neighboring countries.

According to Defense Department budget documents, Kuwait contributed about $210 million per year in similar in-kind support to help defray the costs incurred by the U.S. military personnel that rotated through Kuwait into or out of Iraq for operations in Iraq. In FY2012, Kuwait contributed $350 million for these purposes, as stipulated in the FY2012 Consolidated Appropriation (P.L. 112-74). During 2003-2011, there were an average of 25,000 U.S. troops based in Kuwaiti facilities, not including those rotating into Iraq at a given time. These U.S. forces in Kuwait provided logistical and other support to the U.S. forces moving into or out of Iraq.

U.S. Presence in Kuwait Post-2011

Kuwait served as the key exit route for U.S. troops as they withdrew from Iraq. The United States and Iraq had discussed retaining 3,000-15,000 U.S. troops in Iraq beyond 2011 to continue training Iraqi forces. However, Iraq and the United States were unable to agree on a legal status framework for retaining U.S. troops, and the last U.S. troops left Iraq on December 18, 2011.

Prior to the U.S. withdrawa, there was discussion that the United States might build up forces in Kuwait that could intervene in Iraq if the Iraqi Security Forces run into difficulty.[10] A substantial U.S. force in Kuwait would also presumably add to U.S. capabilities to confront Iran if disputes

---

[10] http://www.worldtribune.com/worldtribune/WTARC/2011/me_iraq1201_09_26.asp; Thom Shanker and Steven Lee Myers. "U.S. Is Planning Buildup in Gulf After Iraq Exit." New York Times, October 30, 2011; Pauline Jelinek, "Kuwait, U.S. Still Talking About Troop Plan." Associated Press, November 7, 2011.

with the United States over its nuclear program and its role in the Middle East and Persian Gulf were to escalate.

Even though violence in Iraq has been escalating since the U.S. departure, there has been no significant increase in U.S. forces in Kuwait. At the time of the withdrawal, deputy National Security Adviser Ben Rhodes told journalists that "There are not really plans to have any substantial increases in any other parts of the Gulf as this war winds down."[11] Then Defense Secretary Leon Panetta noted, in his trip to Kuwait in December 2012, that there were about 13,500 U.S. troops in Kuwait.[12] U.S. force levels are expected to remain at that level for an indefinite period—this force level is higher than that positioned in Kuwait during the 1990s but lower than the 25,000 there for most of the period of U.S. military involvement in Iraq. It also constitutes more than a third of the 35,000 U.S. forces in the Gulf as of late 2013—a figure cited by Defense Secretary Hagel in a trip to the Gulf in December 2013. Some of the U.S. forces currently stationed in Kuwait are combat troops, not purely support forces.[13] This enhanced mix of U.S. forces in Kuwait indicates that the United States wants to retain combat power in close proximity to both Iraq and Iran.

Possibly signaling that Kuwait wants to be fully integrated into post-U.S. withdrawal security structures, including with other U.S. partners, it was reported in December 2011 that NATO discussed with Kuwait opening a center in Kuwait City. This was a follow-on to a decision taken in Istanbul in June 2004 under the "Istanbul Cooperation Initiative (ICI)." Kuwait joined the ICI in December 2004. The NATO center in Kuwait has not opened, to date, in part because the ICI has languished as NATO member states face significant financial constraints.

Kuwait is also cooperating with U.S. efforts to improve the defense capabilities of the GCC as a whole. As noted below, Kuwait is ordering missile defense equipment that supports U.S. efforts to forge a joint GCC missile defense network for the Gulf. At the GCC summit in Kuwait during December 10-11, 2013, Kuwait and the other GCC states announced intent to form a GCC joint military command. The Obama Administration has sought to augment Gulf security in part by forging greater coordination and interoperability of equipment among the GCC states, a decision supported by December 16, 2013 Presidential Determination authorizing U.S. defense sales to the GCC as a whole.

U.S. Security Assistance

Although the threat from Iraq is low compared to what it was during the Saddam era, the United States continues to bolster Kuwait's defense capabilities. U.S. officials say that the U.S.-Kuwait defense relationship, enhanced in recent years by small amounts of U.S. assistance shown in **Table 2** below, has improved the quality of the Kuwaiti military, particularly the air force. Kuwait has received very small amounts of U.S. assistance because of its ability to fund its own security requirements and, as noted above, Kuwait has been mainly a donor to U.S. operations rather than a recipient of U.S. funds. As a result of Kuwaiti recruitment efforts, its military has now nearly regained its pre-Iraq invasion strength of 17,000. In 2008, U.S. Central Command (CENTCOM)

---

[11] "The Cable: Foreign Policy's Josh Rogin." *Washington Post*, December 22, 2011. p. 17.

[12] Thom Shanker. "In Kuwait, Panetta Affirms U.S. Commitment to Middle East. *New York Times*, December 11, 2012.

[13] Michelle Tan. "15,000 in Kuwait, At Least For Now." *Army Times*, January 16, 2012.

established in Kuwait a permanent platform for "full spectrum operations" in 27 countries in the region—among its objectives is to help Kuwait establish a more capable navy.

Arms Sales

U.S. arms sales have sought to enhance Kuwait's capability. In 2010, Kuwait agreed to purchase $1.6 billion in U.S. defense articles and services through the Foreign Military Sales Program. U.S. sales to Kuwait are intended to comport with the overall goals of the "Gulf Security Dialogue" program designed to contain Iran by enhancing the individual and joint capabilities of the Gulf states. Kuwait is not eligible to receive U.S. excess defense articles. Major post-1991 Foreign Military Sales (FMS) include the following:

- 218 M1A2 tanks at a value of $1.9 billion in 1993. Delivery was completed in 1998.

- A 1992 sale of 5 Patriot anti-missile fire units, including 25 launchers and 210 Patriot missiles, valued at about $800 million. Delivery was completed by 1998. Some of them were used to intercept Iraqi short-range missiles launched at Kuwait in the 2003 war.

- A 1992 sale of 40 FA-18 combat aircraft.

- A September 2002 sale of 16 AH-64 (Apache) helicopters equipped with the Longbow fire-control system, valued at about $940 million.

- A December 4, 2007, Defense Security Cooperation Agency (DSCA) notification to Congress reported a sale to Kuwait of 80 PAC-3 (Patriot) missiles and 60 PAC-2 missiles and upgrades, valued at about $1.3 billion.

- On September 9, 2008, DSCA notified a sale of 120 AIM-120C-7 Advanced Medium Range Air-to-Air Missiles (AMRAAM), along with equipment and services, with a total value of $178 million.

- On August 11, 2010, the Administration notified Congress of another potential Patriot-related sale—of 209 Patriot "Guidance Enhanced Missile-T" (GEM-T) missiles valued at $900 million. The prime contractor for that system is Raytheon.

- On February 27, 2012, the Administration notified Congress of a potential sale of 80 AIM-9X-2 SIDEWINDER missiles, and associated parts and support, with an estimated value of $105 million. The sale, if completed, would help Kuwait modernize its fighter aircraft and enhance interoperability with U.S. aircraft.

- On July 20, 2012, the Administration notified a potential sale of 60 Patriot Advanced Capability ("PAC-3") missiles and 20 Patriot launching stations, plus associated equipment. The total value of the sale could reach $4.2 billion. On December 31, 2013, DoD said Lockheed Martin would deliver 14 of the missiles and seven launcher modification kits by June 30, 2016.

- On April 17, 2013, DSCA notified a potential sale to Kuwait of one C-17 cargo aircraft and associated equipment, with an estimated total cost of $371 million.

- On December 4, 2013, DSCA notified a possible sale to Kuwait of technical support to its U.S.-made F-18s for an estimated costs of about $150 million.

- Kuwait is said to be considering adding more FA-18 aircraft, although it is evaluating and might instead order the Rafale or the Typhoon. The latter two combat aircraft are made by European manufacturers.

International Military Education and Training (IMET)

As noted in **Table 2** below, in recent years Kuwait has received very small amounts of funding under the International Military Education and Training (IMET) program. However, Kuwait sends military students to U.S. military institutions to study intelligence, pilot training, and other disciplines. In FY2010, Kuwait spent about $9.7 million to provide such education for 216 Kuwaiti military students. IMET funding that has been provided to Kuwait has been primarily to get Kuwait a discount for Kuwait-funded trainees in U.S. programs. There has been no U.S. assistance to Kuwait since FY2010.

Table 2. U.S. Aid to Kuwait and Purposes

(dollars in thousands)

	FY06	FY07	FY08	FY09	FY10
International Military Training and Education (IMET).	-	19	14	0	10
Non-Proliferation, Anti-Terrorism, De-Mining and Related (NADR).	628	1,025	0	0	0

Foreign Policy Issues

Regional issues were the focus of discussions between the Amir and President Obama on September 13, 2013, according to the White House statement issued after the meeting. After the United States, Kuwait's most important alliance is with the Gulf Cooperation Council (GCC), which consists of fellow Gulf monarchies. In May 2012, Saudi Arabia proposed a close political union among the GCC states—a position that ran into opposition from several GCC states, including Kuwait, and was not adopted. Kuwait has a much longer experience with elections and parliamentary process than does Saudi Arabia or the other GCC states, and most Kuwaitis are perceived as fearful of backsliding on democracy were there to be such a GCC union. The issue was expected to be discussed again at the annual GCC summit on December 10-11, 2013 in Kuwait, but opposition from Oman and others led to a less sweeping GCC announcement to form the joint military command referenced earlier. Kuwait hosted a summit of Afro-Arab countries in November 2013 and will host an Arab League summit meeting in March 2014.

Resolving Residual Bilateral Issues With Iraq

Even though Iraq no longer poses an existential threat to Kuwait, Iraq's stability and the bilateral Iraq-Kuwait relationship remain paramount Kuwaiti foreign policy concerns. Kuwait has tried to build political ties to all Iraqi factions in order to ensure there is no repeat of the 1990 Iraqi invasion of Kuwait or any Iraqi Shiite-led violence such as that which occurred in the 1980s. On July 18, 2008, Kuwait named its first ambassador to Iraq since the 1990 Iraqi invasion—Ali al Momen, a retired general. Momen is a Shiite Muslim, and his appointment signaled Kuwait's acceptance that Iraq is dominated politically by Shiites.

Residual Issues from the 1990 Iraqi Invasion and Occupation

The Kuwait-Iraq relationship remains colored by the August 2, 1990, Iraqi invasion and occupation of Kuwait, which lasted until U.S.-led forces in "Operation Desert Storm" expelled Iraqi forces by February 28, 1991. Relations remained frozen during the rest of Saddam Hussein's rule, and Kuwait remained wary of the post-Saddam Iraqi governments that were dominated by Shiite Muslims. The potential for a major breakthrough in Iraq-Kuwait relations occurred on January 12, 2011, when then Prime Minister Nasser became the first Kuwait Prime Minister to visit Iraq since the Iraqi invasion. Kuwaiti leaders reportedly appreciated the statement by Iraqi Prime Minister Maliki, a few days before the visit, that Iraq's former ambitions against Kuwait "have gone forever and will never return again."[14] These statements set the stage for Iraqi Prime Minister Maliki's first visit to Kuwait on February 16, 2011.

In 2011, some of the mutual suspicions briefly resurfaced. On July 23, 2011, Iraqi parliamentarians called on Kuwait to suspend construction for its Mubarak the Great port because it would impinge on Iraq's attempts to expand its access to the Persian Gulf at the tip of the Faw peninsula. Other parliamentarians alleged that Kuwait was slant drilling in the area and therefore stealing oil from Iraq. The disputes were reminiscent of the arguments made by Saddam Hussein to try to justify his invasion of Kuwait in 1990.

These recriminations quieted, helping resolve some issues during a March 15, 2012, Maliki visit to Kuwait. That visit paved the way for Amir Sabah's attendance at the March 27-29, 2012, Arab League summit in Baghdad—an event Iraq considered crucial to its efforts to return to the Arab fold after decades of isolation. In August 2012, the Iraqi government said "Iraq will end all pending issues with Kuwait before the start of [2013]." The Iraqi statement appeared to be an Iraqi effort to garner support for the U.N. Security Council to remove any remaining "Chapter 7" (of the U.N. Charter) mandates on Iraq stemming from the 1990 invasion. Kuwait's Prime Minister Jaber visited Iraq on June 12, 2013, and reached agreement on taking some of the bilateral issues involving missing Kuwaitis and Kuwaiti property out of the Chapter 7 supervision of the United Nations and replacing them with alternative mechanisms, as discussed below.

Issues Still Outstanding Between Iraq and Kuwait

Reparations Payments Continue. Kuwait has not dropped its insistence on full U.N.-supervised reparations by Iraq for damages caused from the 1990 invasion. Iraq wants the reparations issue closed out to cease the deduction of 5% of all its revenue that is used to pay compensation to the

---

[14] "No Claim on Sovereign Kuwait, Iraqi Ambitions Gone Forever." *Arab Times* (Kuwait). January 9, 2011.

victims of the Iraqi invasion of Kuwait. To date, the U.N. Compensation Commission (UNCC) created by the post-Desert Storm U.N. resolutions has paid out over $38 billion to over 100 governments, encompassing nearly 1.5 million claimants. However, about $13.6 billion is still owed to Kuwaiti claimants, and the U.N. Secretary General's December 14, 2012, report says it expects to complete the compensation process by April 2015. On December 15, 2010, the U.N. Security Council passed three resolutions—1956, 1957, and 1958 that ended Saddam-era sanctions against Iraq, but the resolutions did not end the "Chapter 7" U.N. mandate on Iraq and continued the 5% automatic revenue deductions.

Missing Kuwaitis and Kuwaiti National Archives. The U.N. resolutions adopted December 15, 2010, also continued the effort, required under post-1991 war U.N. resolutions (most notably 687), to resolve the fate of the 605 Kuwaitis and third party nationals missing and presumed dead from the 1991 war, as well as that of the missing Kuwaiti national archives. A special U.N. envoy, Gennady Tarasov, was U.N. High-Level Coordinator for these issues. In September 2011 and in June 2012, Iraq called for an end to the mandate of Tarasov and for Iraq and Kuwait to pursue the issue bilaterally. Tarasov retired on December 31, 2012, and, in the absence of Security Council action on an alternative mechanism, the U.N. Secretary General appointed Victor Poliakov to assume Tarasov's duties.

To date, the search process has resulted in finding the remains of 236 Kuwaitis. The cases of 369 Kuwaitis remain unresolved. In 2010, Kuwait made a $1 million grant to the Iraqi Ministry of Human Rights, which is the lead Iraqi agency trying to determine the fate of the Kuwaitis. A Tripartite Commission on the issue (Kuwait, Iraq, International Committee of the Red Cross) met on May 18, 2011, for the first time in many years. To date, more than 10,000 trenches have been dug to search for remains and jailed members of the Saddam regime have been interviewed. However, the December 14, 2012, and June 17, 2013, U.N. reports on these issues said no progress has been made recently, although some excavations were undertaken in Iraq in 2013.

As far as the Kuwaiti National Archives, U.N. reports on December 14, 2012, and June 17, 2013, say there has been no progress locating the archives. However, Annex I to the June 17, 2013, report (U.N. document S/2013/357) contains a list of all the Kuwaiti property returned to Kuwait by Iraq since 2002. Most recently, in June 2012, Iraq did return to Kuwait numerous boxes of recovered tapes from Kuwait's state radio, as well as books belonging to Kuwait University, and keys to Kuwait's Central Bank.

The June 16, 2013, visit of the Kuwaiti Prime Minister resulted in Iraq-Kuwait joint action to remove these issues of missing property and persons from the Chapter 7 U.N. mandate. That was recommended in the U.N. Secretary General's report of June 17, 2013 (cited above), and contained in U.N. Security Council Resolution 2107 of June 27, 2013. The Resolution formally transferred the continuing supervision of these issues to the U.N. Assistance Mission—Iraq (UNAMI)—under Chapter VI of the U.N. Charter (which does not carry enforcement mechanisms as those adopted under Chapter VII).

Kuwait-Iraq Border. Disputes over the Iraq-Kuwait border have also been mostly resolved. Under post-1991 Gulf War U.N. Security Council Resolution 833, the Council accepted the U.N.-demarcated border between them. Kuwait has sought that the post-Saddam government in Iraq formally acknowledge its commitments under the resolution to pay some of the costs of border markings and signs. In July 2010, Kuwait gave preliminary approval to open a special border crossing into Iraq that would facilitate the work of international oil companies working in Iraq. And, as a consequence of the March 15, 2012, Maliki visit to Kuwait, Iraq agreed to pay its portion of the costs of maintaining the border markings. The issue of the sea border markings and related issues was resolved in early 2013. The resolution of these issues led Kuwait to support the termination of the High Level Coordinator mandate on the missing Kuwaiti persons and property issue discussed above.

Other Outstanding Bilateral Disputes/Iraqi Airways. Among other residual issues from the Saddam era, in 2004, Kuwait reportedly pledged to forgive a substantial portion of the $25 billion Saddam era debt, but it has not written off the debt to date. Another major dispute concerned Kuwait Airways' lawsuits alleging that Iraq owed Kuwait $1.2 billion for planes and parts stolen during the Iraqi invasion; the actions led to the long-term impoundment of Iraqi Airways jets. The March 15, 2012, Maliki visit resolved the issue with agreement for Iraq to pay Kuwait $300 million in compensation, and to invest $200 million in an Iraq-Kuwait joint venture to form a small new airline. Subsequent to the visit, Iraq-Kuwait direct flights resumed. In November 2013, Kuwait's national airline, Kuwait Airways, made its first flight to Iraq (Najaf) since the 1990 Iraqi invasion.

Remaining Threat from Iraqi Extremist Groups. Even though Iraq and Kuwait have improved relations to a degree many experts did not think possible, violence emanating from extremist groups in Iraq is a threat to Kuwait. The December 1983 bombings of the U.S. and French embassies in Kuwait and an attempted assassination of the Amir in May 1985 were attributed to the Iran-inspired Iraqi Da'wa (Islamic Call) Party. This is the party that Iraqi Prime Minister Nuri al-Maliki heads, although the party no longer has a militia wing. Seventeen Da'wa activists were arrested for these attacks, and Da'wa activists hijacked a Kuwait Airlines plane in 1987. In July 2011, an Iraqi Shiite militia supported by Iran (the militia of cleric Moqtada Al Sadr) rocketed Kuwait's embassy in Iraq and caused Kuwait to temporarily bring its diplomats back to Kuwait. In July 2011, another Iraqi Shiite militia, Khata'ib Hezbollah, threatened to attack workers building the Mubarak the Great port (named after a past ruler) on Bubiyan Island, as discussed below. These and other Iraqi Shiite militias continue to operate in southern Iraq, and a munition was fired into Kuwaiti territory in August 2011, but these Shiite groups are said to be evolving into political movements and de-emphasizing their armed wings.

Iran

For the years after the Iraqi invasion, Kuwait supported Iran as a potential counterweight to Saddam Hussein. Kuwait often hosted pro-Iranian Iraqi Shiite oppositionists against Saddam, even though these same Shiite groups had conducted attacks in Kuwait in the 1980s, as noted. Since Saddam's fall, Kuwait has largely joined U.S. efforts to contain Iran and to enact strict international sanctions to compel it to curb its nuclear program. In May 2010, Kuwait confirmed that it had arrested some Kuwaiti civil servants and stateless residents for allegedly working on behalf of the Qods (Jerusalem) Force of the Islamic Revolutionary Guard Corps (IRGC) of Iran in a plot to blow up Kuwaiti energy facilities.[15] (The Qods Force, named as a terrorism supporting entity by the United States, is the IRGC unit that supports pro-Iranian movements and conducts espionage in neighboring and other foreign countries.) The Qods Force activity in Kuwait suggested that Iran might be looking to pressure Kuwait because of its alliance with the United States. In March 2011, a Kuwait court sentenced two Iranians and a Kuwaiti to death in the

---

[15] "Iran Spy Cell Dismantled in Kuwait." Associated Press, May 6, 2010; "Iran Cell Planned Attacks in Kuwait, Minister Says. *Reuters*, April 21, 2011.

alleged plot. Kuwait expelled three Iranian diplomats, and Iran expelled three Kuwaiti diplomats in response. The sentences were commuted to life in prison on May 28, 2012. In May 2011, the two countries agreed to return their respective ambassadors. In November 2011, Iran arrested several individuals in Iran who it alleged were "Kuwaiti spies."

Kuwait also is cooperating with the growing global consensus to sanction Iran. This cooperation has come despite the comments by the Amir in November 2009 endorsing Iran's right to purely peaceful nuclear energy. In July 2010, a U.S. law, P.L. 111-195 (the Comprehensive Iran Sanctions, Accountability, and Divestment Act of 2010) was enacted that would penalize firms that supply gasoline to Iran. A Kuwaiti gasoline trading firm, Kuwait's Independent Petroleum Group, was reported to be a supplier of gasoline to Iran,[16] although the firm told U.S. officials it stopped doing so as of September 2010. In September 2012, Kuwaiti naval forces—as well as those of all the Gulf Cooperation Council states—participated in U.S.-led mine clearing exercises in the Persian Gulf—exercises apparently intended to signal to Iran the strength of a U.S.-led coalition to contain Iran. As noted, Kuwait is also buying U.S. missile defense equipment as part of the U.S. effort to defend the Gulf against Iran's missile capabilities.

Arab-Israeli Dispute

For many years after the Iraqi invasion, the positions taken by countries and factions on how to deal with the Iraqi invasion determined Kuwait's foreign relations. Kuwait was more critical than were the other Gulf states of the late Palestinian leader Yasir Arafat because he had opposed war to liberate Kuwait from Iraq. Kuwait expelled about 450,000 Palestinian workers after liberation, viewing them as disloyal. Kuwait subsequently maintained ties and gave financial support to Arafat's Palestinian antagonist, Hamas. Kuwait's relations with Jordan was strained for many years because of then leader King Hussein's opposition to a U.S.-led war to expel Iraqi forces from Kuwait. In recent years, the Iraq issue has faded in Kuwait's foreign relations decisions.

In part because of Kuwait's past antagonism to the mainstream Palestine Liberation Organization (PLO) that still largely leads the Palestinian Authority (PA), Kuwait has not been a major mediator in intra-Palestinian disputes. Nor has it publicly advanced its own proposals for resolving the Israeli-Palestinian dispute. In line with the positions of the other GCC and Arab states, Kuwait supports U.N. recognition of the State of Palestine, requested formally by PA President Mahmoud Abbas at the U.N. General Assembly meetings in September 2011.

During the period of active Gulf-Israel negotiations (1992-1997), Kuwait attended multilateral working group peace talks with Israel—sessions on arms control, water resources, refugees, and other issues that were begun as part of the "Oslo Accords process" between Israel and the Palestinians. However, Kuwait did not host any sessions of the multilaterals. In 1994, Kuwait was key in persuading the other Gulf monarchies to cease enforcement of the secondary (trade with firms that deal with Israel) and tertiary (trade with firms that do business with blacklisted firms) Arab boycotts of Israel. However, Kuwait did not, as did Qatar and Oman, subsequently exchange trade offices with Israel, amounting to a renunciation of the primary boycott (boycott on direct trade with Israel).

---

[16] http://www.defenddemocracy.org/index.php?option=com_content&task=view&id=11788115&Itemid=105.

Positions and Actions on 2011 Uprisings Elsewhere in the Region

Kuwait has generally acted in concert with—although not necessarily identically to—the other GCC states on the uprisings in the Middle East that began in 2011. These GCC actions and initiatives have generally coincided with U.S. interests, such as in Syria.

Bahrain. Of all the countries affected by "Arab spring" demonstrations, Kuwait has paid the closest attention to the situation in Bahrain, which is a fellow GCC member. Kuwait sent a naval unit to support the March 14, 2011, intervention of the GCC's "Peninsula Shield" unit to assist Bahraini security forces. The nearly 2,000 GCC ground forces that entered Bahrain were Saudi troops and UAE police. The Kuwaiti naval unit returned to Kuwait in July 2011 following the end of the state of emergency there. The GCC intervention was at odds with U.S. policy to support dialogue between Bahrain's government and protesters and avoid repression. The Kuwaiti intervention also put the Sabah government at odds with Kuwaiti Shiites. At the risk of Kuwaiti Shiite criticism, then-Prime Minister Nasser visited Bahrain during July 9, 2011.

Libya. Kuwait supported the Arab League position in favor of U.N.-mandated intervention to protect civilians but, initially, it stopped short of recognizing the Transitional National Council (TNC) as the legitimate representative of the Libyan people (an action that Qatar and the UAE took). In April 2011, it pledged about $177 million in financial aid to the TNC. Kuwait did not contribute any air or other forces to the NATO coalition that conducted strikes in support of anti-Qadhafi rebels. It recognized the TNC as the sole legitimate representative after the fall of Tripoli in August 2011.

Yemen. As a GCC state, Kuwait cooperated with developing and implementing the GCC plan for a peaceful transition of power in Yemen. That effort bore fruit with the departure of President Ali Abdullah Saleh in January 2012 and the subsequent presidential elections in March 2012.

Syria. In part because Syrian President Bashar Al Assad is aligned with Iran, Kuwait and the other GCC want Assad ousted. The GCC countries voted with other Arab League countries to suspend Syria's membership in that body in November 2011, and they all closed their embassies there entirely by April 2012. Also in April 2012, the GCC states proposed providing $100 million in funding to the armed opposition, and Kuwait is reported to be contributing funds, but apparently not arms, to the Syrian rebels. On January 30, 2013, Kuwait hosted a major donors' meeting to aid Syrian civilian victims of the conflict; $1.5 billion was pledged at that meeting, including $300 million from Kuwait. In April 2013, Kuwait pledged another $300 million in humanitarian aid for the Syria crisis—$275 million to nine U.N. agencies and $25 million to the International Committee of the Red Cross (ICRC). Kuwait hosted another donors conference for Syria humanitarian aid on January 15, 2014, and it made the largest pledge ($500 million) of any country at the meeting. (In total, $2.4 billion was pledged there.)

The United States and other countries reportedly are concerned about reported efforts by wealthy Kuwaitis to contribute funds to certain hardline Islamist Syrian rebel factions.[17] According to press reports, Kuwaiti donors and donor aggregators use social media and other methods to collect funds for such Syrian factions as Al Nusra Front, which the U.S. government asserts is an affiliate of Al Qaeda.[18] It is not clear whether any Kuwaitis are donating to the Islamic State of

---

[17] Joby Warrick, "Wealthy Donors Influence Syria War," *Washington Post*, June 16, 2013.

[18] Ben Hubbard. "Donors' Funds Add Wild Card to War in Syria." New York Times, November 13, 2013.

Iraq and Syria (ISIS) faction which has a stronger affiliation with Al Qaeda than does Al Nusra. The total amounts of such Kuwaiti donations to Syrian rebel groups is not know. U.S. officials reportedly are urging the Kuwaiti government to try to stop this financial flow, but without any evident result to date. The Kuwaiti government, as well as the donors involved, purportedly do not consider the Syrian rebel factions as "terrorists" to which funds should be denied.

Egypt. Kuwait has adopted a position at odds with some of the other GCC states, particularly Qatar. Qatar was the major Gulf financial benefactor of Egypt during the presidency of Muslim Brotherhood senior figure Mohammad Morsi. However, Kuwait is aligned with another GCC state, the United Arab Emirates (UAE), in its wariness of the Brotherhood. Kuwaiti leaders assert that the Muslim Brotherhood in Egypt supports Muslim Brotherhood oppositionists in Kuwait. Kuwait did not aid Morsi's government during his rule and, after Morsi was deposed by the Egyptian military on July 3, 2013, both Kuwait and the UAE announced large financial pledges to help the beleaguered Egyptian economy. Kuwait announced it would give Egypt a $2 billion loan; a $1 billion grant; and a grant of $1 billion worth of oil and other petroleum products[19] as part of a Saudi-brokered package for Egypt totaling $12 billion. Kuwaiti leaders have been somewhat critical of U.S. cuts in aid to Egypt since the Morsi ouster, as reportedly was discussed during the White House meeting on September 13, 2013, between the Amir and President Obama.

Kuwait has also made arrests of Egyptians in Kuwait for political activities. In April 2011, just after President Hosni Mubarak was overthrown, security officers arrested and deported 21 Egyptian nationals resident in Kuwait for attending meetings in support of Egyptian opposition figure Dr. Mohammad El Baradei. In August 2011, in line with Kuwait's stance against the Egyptian Muslim Brotherhood, Kuwaiti authorities said they would deport nine pro-Morsi demonstrators who had been protesting outside the Egyptian embassy in Kuwait.

Other Assistance. In July 2011, Kuwait contributed $1 million to help relieve the effects of drought in Somalia. In November 2013, Kuwait donated $10 million in relief aid to the Philippines following a destructive typhoon there.

Kuwaiti Cooperation Against Islamic Militancy[20]

Notwithstanding concerns over private Kuwaiti donations to hardline Islamist factions in Syria, the State Department report on global terrorism for 2012 (released May 30, 2013) credited Kuwaiti leaders with maintaining efforts to counter terrorism and violent extremism. The praise was extended despite the lack of a clear legal framework in Kuwait for prosecuting terrorism-related crimes or terrorism financing. There were no significant attacks attributed to terrorist or terrorist organizations in Kuwait in 2012, according to the report, and press reports do not indicate that there were any such attacks in 2013. On November 27, 2011, security services arrested three Kuwaiti military officials on suspicion of links with a terrorist cell plotting to attack locations in Bahrain and Qatar. Pro-Iranian groups and agents are in Kuwait are discussed in the sections above on Iran and Iraq.

Kuwait is a member of the Middle East North Africa Financial Action Task Force (FATF), but it has been identified by that body as having deficiencies in combating terrorism financing. Kuwait

---

[19] "Kuwait Offers Egypt $4B Aid, Fuel Package." Associated Press, July 10, 2013.

[20] For the 2012 State Department country report on terrorism, see http://www.state.gov/j/ct/rls/crt/2012/209982 htm.

has developed an action plan with the FATF to address the weaknesses. Some Kuwait-based organizations have proved problematic in the past. On June 13, 2008, the Treasury Department froze the assets of a Kuwaiti charity with alleged links to Al Qaeda—the Revival of Islamic Heritage Society—under Executive Order 13224. Past State Department terrorism reports have praised Kuwait's programs to encourage moderation in Islam in Kuwait.

In April 2011 Kuwait introduced biometric fingerprinting at Kuwait International Airport and has since extended that system to land and sea entry points. The NADR funds shown above have been used, in large part, to assist Kuwait with counterterrorism efforts, border control, and export controls.

Kuwait seeks the return of two prisoners held at the U.S. facility in Guantanamo Bay, Cuba, under accusation of belonging to Al Qaeda. Amir Sabah reportedly raised the issue with President Obama during their September 13, 2013, White House meeting. Kuwait has built a rehabilitation center for the two, Fayez al Kandari and Fawzi al-Udah, to reintegrate them into society after they are returned. The Obama Administration has said it shares the goal of returning them to Kuwait.[21]

Kuwaiti Economic Policy

The political turmoil in Kuwait since 2006 has had economic costs. Executive-legislative disputes delayed passage of stimulus measures to address the effects in Kuwait of the 2008-2009 global financial crisis. As the crisis has abated, the National Assembly passed some legislation, which took effect September 2010, to privatize major sectors of the Kuwait economy. In January 2014, the National Assembly approved legislation to privatize Kuwait Airways. Some Kuwaitis, particularly those newly naturalized and less affluent than longtime citizens, expressed concerns that privatization of Kuwait Airways and other major state-owned companies would bring higher unemployment.

In part because of the political disputes and 2011-2013 unrest, Kuwait has underinvested in capital infrastructure and overspent on public sector salaries and subsidies, according to the IMF and other observers. The Kuwaiti budgets in 2011-13 appeared intended to calm or avoid unrest rather than to set Kuwait up for long-term growth. As an example of government largesse, in mid-2013, the National Assembly passed a law obligating the government to pay $2.5 billion in debts owed by Kuwaitis as a result of the 2008 financial crisis. Total subsidies cost the government about $17.7 billion annually. Observers say that the government benefits, if continued at current rates, are likely to put Kuwait's budget into deficit during 2017-2020. In response to those projections, in late October 2013 Prime Minister Jaber said the subsidies system had produced a "welfare state" and was "unsustainable," and he pledged to work to reduce them.

Delayed spending on capital infrastructure projects has at least temporarily avoided putting the national budget into deficit, but has also created an image of stagnation, particularly compared to the more vibrant GCC states Qatar and UAE. This impression has been augmented by a lag in foreign direct investment in Kuwait relative to other GCC states. Only $800 million has been

---

[21] Darlene Superville. "Kuwait Ruler Presses Obama on Guantanamo Detainees." Miami Herald, September 14, 2013.

invested in Kuwait in the past 10 years. In contrast, in the same time period, $10 billion was invested in Bahrain, $73 billion in UAE, and $130 billion in Saudi Arabia.[22]

The political deadlock in Kuwait has also prevented movement on several major potential drivers of future growth, the most prominent of which is Project Kuwait. The project, backed by the Kuwaiti government, would open Kuwait's northern oil fields to foreign investment to generate about 500,000 barrels per day of extra production. The Assembly has blocked the $8.5 billion project for over a decade because of concerns about Kuwait's sovereignty, and observers say no compromise is in sight. A project to build a fourth oil refinery, estimated to cost $8 billion, also has not advanced.

The 2008 financial crisis, coupled with the political infighting, also caused Kuwait to shelve a joint venture with Dow Chemical to form the largest maker of polyethylene. On December 29, 2008, the government cancelled the venture, which was to have required a Kuwaiti investment of $7.5 billion by state-run Petrochemical Industries Co.-Kuwait. Dow reportedly had planned to use the proceeds of the investment to fund its purchase of the Rohm and Haas chemical firm, although that deal ultimately went through anyway. In May 2013, an arbitrator decided in favor of Dow Chemical, ordering the Petrochemical Industries Co.-Kuwait to pay Dow $2.2 billion in damages for severing the venture.

The state-owned oil industry still accounts for 75% of government income and 90% of export earnings. The United States imports about 250,000 barrels per day in crude oil from Kuwait (about 3% of U.S. oil imports). Total U.S. exports to Kuwait were about $2.7 billion in 2012, the same as the few preceding years, consisting mostly of automobiles, industrial equipment, and foodstuffs. Total U.S. imports from Kuwait in 2012 were about $13 billion, of which almost all was crude oil and other petroleum products. Figures available from January through November of 2013 indicate that U.S.-Kuwait trade for all of 2013 was at roughly the same level as 2012.

Like other Gulf states, Kuwait sees peaceful uses of nuclear energy as important to its economy, although doing so always raises fears among some in the United States, Israel, and elsewhere about the ultimate intentions of developing a nuclear program. Kuwait is cooperating with the International Atomic Energy Agency (IAEA) to ensure international oversight of any nuclear work in Kuwait.

In 1994, Kuwait became a founding member of the World Trade Organization (WTO). In February 2004, the United States and Kuwait signed a Trade and Investment Framework Agreement (TIFA), often viewed as a prelude to a free trade agreement (FTA), which Kuwait has said it seeks. Kuwait gave $500 million worth of oil to U.S. states affected by Hurricane Katrina.

---

[22] "Kuwait in Crisis As Ruling Family Splits, MP's Rebel." *Reuters*, June 7, 2011.

Table 3. Some Basic Facts

Leadership	Amir: Shaykh Sabah al-Ahmad al-Jabir Al Sabah. Crown Prince/heir apparent: Shaykh Nawwaf al-Ahmad al-Jabir Al Sabah. Prime Minister: Shaykh Jabir al-Mubarak Al Sabah
Population	About 2.7 million, of which 1.4 million are citizens.
GDP (purchasing power parity, PPP)	$166 billion (2012)
Religions	Muslim 85% (Sunni 70%, Shiite 30%); other (Christian, Hindu, Parsi) 15%
GDP per capita (PPP)	$43,800/yr (2012)
GDP growth rate	6.3% (2012)
Inflation	3.2% (2012)
Oil (proven reserves)	102 billion barrels (7% of world proven reserves)
Oil exports	2.15 million barrels per day (mbd)

Sources: CRS; CIA, *The World Factbook* reports; IMF.

Figure 1. Map of Kuwait

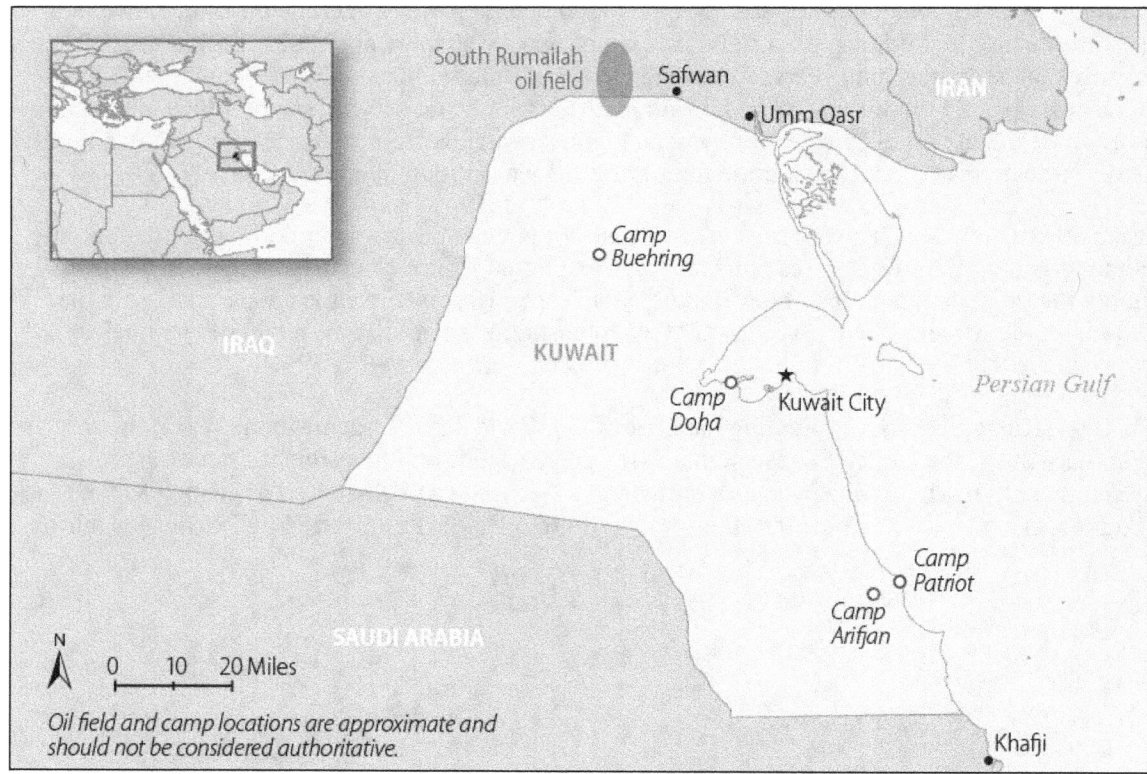

Source: Graphic created by CRS. Boundaries and cities generated by Hannah Fischer using data from Department of State, Esri, and Google Maps (all 2013).

Author Contact Information

Kenneth Katzman
Specialist in Middle Eastern Affairs
kkatzman@crs.loc.gov, 7-7612

www.ingramcontent.com/pod-product-compliance
Lightning Source LLC
Chambersburg PA
CBHW080752290526
45790CB00008B/3423